MW01291891

The Cemetery by Scott Bosek

ISBN: 978-1548708115

THE CEMETERY

By Scott Bosek

Illustrated by

Emily Allar

STORIES FROM MR. B

This story as well as the others from the series entitled " Stories from Mr. B," are taken from my childhood memories of growing up in a close knit neighborhood in Detroit during the 1960's and as far as I can remember, are all true. Even though many of the people in these stories have long since passed away, I felt it necessary to change some of their names in order to respect their privacy. I began telling these stories while substitute teaching. When my students finished with their lessons and there was extra time left in the day, these stories were a great way to fill the time. Many of my friends and family have been asking me to write them down. These books are the result. I hope you enjoy reading them as much as I enjoy remembering them.

Mr. B

" Hey Mr. B, if we get our work done could you please tell us one of your stories?"

"Well if we get our work done and if you guys behave yourselves, then I guess that would be fine. Which one would you like to hear?"

" How about.....

Contents

PREFACE

Cemeteries mean different things to different people. Some view them as scary places and do not want to go anywhere near them. Others find them to be a peaceful place where they can go to enjoy a quiet break from the noise of the city. Yet still others find them to be a place of reverence – a holy place where loved ones are remembered. I have a friend who is the pastor of a church and he often goes to the cemetery to pray. Whatever your feelings are about cemeteries, after reading this book you will never look at them the same again. I hope you enjoy the adventure.

Chapter One

The Farm

Up until the year my father died, my family spent nearly every weekend during the summer helping my grandparents work their farm. It was always grandma and grandpa's dream to own a farm. When they came to America from Poland they began saving their money, unfortunately by the time they had enough money to buy a farm they were quite old and needed help working it - and that's where we came in. Most weekends during the summer and fall we went to the farm where my parents, along with my uncles and aunts, helped with the chores. There were eighty acres where they grew corn, beans and wheat. An acre is about the size of a football field so there was a lot of room for my cousins and I to play. The farm was located in a small town in the lower part of Michigan's thumb area called Jeddo. My dad had 5 brothers and sisters and they also helped my grandparents work the farm, so there were always a lot of cousins to play with.

I had a lot of cousins but my favorite was Kim. Kim was a bit of a tomboy and she could do pretty much anything I could do. We were very competitive, often racing each other to see who was faster. The farm had cows, chickens, pigs and even a few horses. Next to the farmhouse was an apple orchard and smack dab in the middle of the orchard stood an old rusty swing set. My cousins and I spent hours on that swing set, never keeping track of time. I can still hear the chains creaking as we competed to see who could swing the highest.

When the corn was at its tallest in late August and ready to be harvested, my brother and I would take walks through the cornfield pretending that we were hiding from enemy soldiers. Sometimes we would walk so far into the cornfield that we would get lost. It would sometimes take us hours to find our way out, but that was OK, we never kept track of time and it was so much fun. Except when the dragonflies chased us. I was deathly afraid of dragonflies!

Despite its haunted house appearance and the dozens of spider webs, my Grandpa's old tool shed was another place we liked to play. My brother and I would pretend we were repairing things – like a broken wagon or tractor engine – just like my grandpa did. When he caught us playing in the shed grandpa would always shoo us out yelling: "You boys stay out of that tool shed or else!" None of us wanted to find out what "or else" meant. By far our very favorite place to play was inside the barn. That's where grandpa parked his big green tractor. The tires on his tractor were twice as tall as we were! We would climb up on the tractor, sit behind the wheel and pretend we were plowing the fields – just like grandpa and my dad did. My dad used to let me sit on his lap and steer the tractor for the short ride down the dirt road that led to a farm on the corner. There, we delivered the big cans of milk. From there a semi-truck would come once a week to pick up all the milk that the farmers in the area had produced. Then it was off to the milk company the cans would go. The milk truck driver would leave each farmer their money in separate envelopes according to how many gallons of milk they left. Each can held 10 gallons. And that's how the farmers got paid.

Back to the barn; if my grandpa caught us playing on his tractor we would really be in trouble. He would say: "Boys, if I told you once I told you a thousand times stay off my tractor – now you get in the house and tell grandma that I said no apple pie tonight!"

Chapter Two

Grandma's Cooking

We seemed to have apple pie for desert a lot on the farm. I guess it was because everybody loved it and because there were plenty of apples available for free! Now dinner without apple pie may not seem like much of a punishment to you but then again you have never tasted my grandma's cooking. Grandma made *the best* bread, most awesome canned peaches and of course – apple pie that was out of this world! What was amazing to me was how she could do so using her very old wood burning stove. Many a time I sat and watched as she would monitor the temperature of the oven using the little thermostat that was mounted on the front of the stove. To increase the temperature, she simply lifted one of the iron disks on the stovetop and added another log. The bread was so good that when we got home I would hide it so that no one else would eat it but me!

There was one place on the farm that we had not yet explored. Out beyond the cow pasture was a small patch of woods. We often talked about going there but my older cousin Linda had told us to stay away because it was haunted and that if we disturbed the ghost of the woods it would come and haunt the farmhouse! So naturally we stayed away.

Chapter Three

The Woods

As we got older and a little braver, we decided one day that we were going to have an adventure to the woods and see if our older cousin was telling the truth. So, my cousin Kim, my kid brother Rob and I got up very early one morning – before anyone else was awake and headed for the woods. It was a long walk and we always had to be careful not to step in those nasty cow pies.

When we finally got to the outer edge of the woods and looked in, it seemed very dark and scary. Under the canopy of trees it was a different world. The air was cool and calm and it was very quiet. We slowly entered the woods and just as we began exploring, my cousin Kim suddenly yelled out *"look over there!"* We looked to our left and to our amazement saw a very old cemetery! Not many gravestones, maybe 30 or so. Just then I remembered what my older cousin Linda had told us and thought to myself "maybe this place really is haunted."

We began clearing the dirt off the grave markers to see what they said. These were some very old tombstones. One said ***James Smith, beloved husband, died after falling off his tractor: born 1830 died 1857***. "Why that was before the Civil War!" I said.

Another one said **Here lies Chase Williams, sheriff of Jeddo, died in the line of duty. Born 1841, died 1875**. "He may have *fought* in the Civil War!"

"Look, this is an area where they buried the children" Kim said. Rob asked why so many kids died at a such a young age. I told him that it was because they did not have the medicines we have today, so many children died before their time. Just then we heard it - the most terrifying sound we'd ever heard! *SCREEEECH, SCREEEECH – it was the ghost!* I turned around to see Rob and Kim running as fast as they could towards the cow pasture. I yelled "wait for me!" And I was right behind them.

Chapter Four

The Ghost

We ran all the way back to the farm, jumped over the fence and landed on our backs in the deep grass, panting and trembling with fear. "The woods really are haunted" I said.

"Yeah, and now we went and disturbed the ghost" Kim said.

Just then our older cousin Linda came walking past and asked us what was going on. We told her what we had done and she stared at us in disbelief. "You're kidding me, right?" she said.

"Do we look like we are kidding?" I yelled.

"Now you've done it", she said. "If something isn't done quickly that ghost will be here before you know it."

"What do you mean if something isn't done? "Wait a minute, you mean something can be done to stop it?" I said.

"Not only stop it, but send it back to where it came from." She said.

"And how are we supposed to do that – scare it back?"

"No goofball, grandma told me a long time ago that if the ghost is ever disturbed we would need to put a clove of garlic in a jar of water and set it in the woods by the graveyard, that would send the ghost back to wherever it came from."

"You're kidding, right?" I said.

"Nope, and you'd better do it soon or the ghost of the woods will soon be at our farmhouse door!" As Linda walked away,

Kim and I began to hatch a plan that would send the ghost of the woods back to where it came from – wherever that was.

Chapter Five

The Plan

Kim told me that she knew right where grandma kept her garlic and that as soon as everyone was in bed that she would borrow a clove for our concoction. That meant I had the unfortunate task of finding a jar, unfortunate because the jars were down in the cellar also known as - *The Dungeon*. Whenever grandma was ready to can her famous peaches, she would have me go down in the cellar and bring up the mason jars that were stored there. I always dreaded going down in that cellar for three reasons. One, there was only one light and it was at the bottom of the steep narrow steps.

Two, here were always plenty of spider webs along the walls that led to the dungeon like cellar. It even had a dirt floor, what people used to call a "Michigan basement." And thirdly, although I never saw one, I knew there were rats down there. While getting the jars I had always noticed that there were several rat traps set up, and if there were rat traps there must have been rats. We once saw a dead rat the size of a cat sprawled out on top of a grain pile inside old Vooyah's barn. Vooyah means "uncle" in Polish. He was my grandma's brother and quite a character. Vooyah was an old man and owned the farm down the road from us. He had a finger missing due to an accident he had while sharpening his ax. We kids always asked him to show us his missing finger and tell us about the accident. Vooyah told us that the rat we saw probably had eaten himself to death! None the less, the cellar was where the mason jars were and it was now my job to get one so that we could complete our concoction.

When everyone was asleep I tiptoed down the steps, through the kitchen and to the cellar door. I slowly opened the door and using my Cub Scout flashlight, made my way down the steps. The steps seemed even more narrow and steep than the last time I was there. I could see a few spider webs and one had a huge spider sitting in the middle of the web just waiting for its prey. I walked down the steps as slowly and quietly as I could, all the while keeping my eyes on the spider until I finally reached the dirt floor.

The mason jars were stacked in the corner. I stomped my feet a few times to scare any rats away and grabbed a jar, then quickly headed back up the stairs and back to the bedroom. Kim had already gotten the garlic so we put the clove into the jar of water, screwed the lid on it and placed it carefully under the bed. We set the alarm for 5 a.m. and tried to get some sleep.

Chapter Six

Back into the Woods

The next morning when we woke up, we quietly got dressed and tiptoed down the steps, through the kitchen and out the door. The sun was just coming up as we headed out to the cow pasture. As we climbed over the fence and began the long walk to the woods I could tell that we were walking much slower than we had the time before. Neither of us were in a hurry to go back into those woods. We could see the trees now that the sun was coming up and they had an eerie look to them, almost as if they were warning us to stay away. As we got closer

Kim said, "I really don't want to go back in there."

I said, "I don't either but we have to do this or things will only get worse."

She agreed and we continued our slow walk toward the woods. We finally reached the outer edge and stopped. It seemed even quieter and colder than the last time we were there. We stepped in and began walking towards the cemetery. Had it not been for what we were facing, the woods seemed like a cool place to explore. Kim was not the quietest of walkers and I had to keep telling her to walk softly and to avoid the dead leaves and sticks that crackled under her feet. Then we saw our destination and both looked at each other with fear. "The faster we do this the faster we can get the heck out of here," Kim said. I quickly took the lid off the jar and we gently set it down in the middle of the headstones.

No sooner had I set the jar down when we heard it again - that terrifying – *SCREEEECH, SCREEEECH* - like before, off we ran. We shot out of the woods and all the way across the cow pasture till we reached the fence. Kim jumped right over the fence but I struggled and ended up crawling under it. So, there we were again gasping for breath, congratulating each other over our accomplishment.

Chapter Seven

Mission Accomplished

We did it! The farm was safe and we vowed *never* to return to the woods again. Just then, grandma came walking by with a basket full of fresh eggs. She asked us what we were doing. As I began telling her the whole story of how we managed to release and then return the ghost of the woods back to it's rest, she began to smile and soon did something grandma rarely did – she started laughing. Louder and louder until I finally asked: "I don't understand, what's so funny grandma?"

"You kids have been hoodwinked," she said.

"Hoodwinked, what's that?" I asked.

"You know - tricked, fooled" she said.

She said that my cousin Linda had made the whole ghost story up to keep us from wandering too far from the farmhouse. None of it was true she said. "But grandma," Kim said, "we heard it as plain as we hear you – it was real I tell you."

"Follow me" she said.

Grandma set her eggs down, grabbed our hands, and off we went walking towards the woods again.

Chapter Eight

Here We Go Again

There was a gate a little way down that made it much easier to get to the cow pasture – we just never saw it. "Grandma," I said, why are you taking us back to the woods?"

"To show you your so-called ghost,"she said.

There was no way we wanted to go back to the cemetery but grandma was holding our hands - and when grandma held your hand, you didn't let go until she said so. When we reached the woods Kim and I tried to hold grandma back but she just turned to us with a smile and said; "quit being such scaredy cats." In we went for the third time. When we reached the cemetery she pointed to the jar we had set down and laughed and said, "Is that what you thought would get rid of your ghost?" Just then our conversation was interrupted by a *SCREEEEECH*. It was the ghost, the concoction didn't work! As we tried to run grandma just held us tighter and said "Look – is this what you thought was your ghost?" Pointing to a large oak tree smack dab in the middle of the cemetery and in the crook of the tree sat an owl.

Grandma said that it was a barred owl. Boy, were we ever relieved there wasn't really a ghost! Again, it called out – *SCREEEEECH.* Grandma said, "that old

mama owl probably has babies in a nest up there and it's warning you to stay away - that's all, so you see, it ain't no ghost, just a mother owl who is probably just as scared as you are."

Chapter Nine

A (History) Lesson to Be Learned

I asked grandma why there was a cemetery on our farm and who all the people were who were buried there. She explained to Kim and I that in the old days, cemeteries were sometimes so far away that when a family member died they would start their own family plot on their land. As time went by and neighbors had loved ones pass away, they asked the family if they could bury their relative in the cemetery. That's how it grew and why there were all kinds of different people buried there. The cemetery was already on the farm when grandma and grandpa bought it. They always respected the families who had loved ones buried there so they left it alone. "You should always show respect for the dead, always remember that," she said. "No matter what a person had done in this life, if they made peace with God at the end then they would be in heaven." I remembered those words and always felt that even the worst people could have a chance to be with God after they died. As we left the woods and the cemetery behind, grandma told us about the stories she had heard from the old timers who said that some of the men buried there did indeed serve in the Civil War and that Chase Williams – sheriff of Jeddo – really did die in a gunfight during a bank robbery. What a cool history lesson! We finally got back to the gate and grandma picked up her basket of eggs and said, "Now, let's go back to the farmhouse, I think there is some leftover apple pie." As we headed for the house I said "Ya know, I knew all along that it was an owl making that noise, I was just playing along to see how scared you would be." Grandma and Kim looked at me and said, "*sure* you did."

Chapter Ten

The Sad Discovery

Twenty-five years had passed when I received a phone call from my sister who was living in California. She wanted to send her two girls to visit and was hoping I would take them to see the farm. Shortly after my dad passed away my grandparents sold the farm. They were just too old to keep up with the work required to run it. I hadn't been back since then and I just assumed everything was pretty much the same except for the owners, so I said sure I'd be happy to take them. Trouble was I'd forgotten how to get there. I called my Aunt Mary who was the matriarch of the family and asked her for directions. To my surprise she said: "Why didn't you know, the farm isn't there anymore, it burned down years ago." I couldn't believe it, I was so upset – why hadn't anyone told me? Well, I still wanted to take my nieces to the place where it once was, and hopefully the cemetery was still there. So early one Saturday morning we set out for the farm, or what was left of it. When we arrived not only was the farm gone but a new house had been built on the property. No barn, no chicken coop, no tool shed and worst of all – no woods! I was heartbroken. I tried to explain to the girls what the farm once looked like but it just wasn't the same. Then I remembered, a set of railroad tracks ran right next to the woods. As kids, we loved the railroad tracks. We would put coins on the tracks so when the train ran them over they would flatten out and take on a whole new look. The trains always seemed to come at night. When we heard the whistle, we would look out our window and see the light on the front of the engine.

I thought that If I could find the tracks there was a chance I could find the cemetery. We drove a little way down the dirt road and there they were! We got out of my car and began to walk down the tracks to where I thought the woods once stood. There was a steep gully running parallel to the tracks and after walking a bit I saw a large patch of bushes with several old tree stumps among them. I descended the gully and as I got closer I couldn't believe my eyes. There it was – or I should say what was left of – the cemetery. The tombstones were broken and smashed, broken bottles and cigarette butts lay strewn about. This was done deliberately by what I guessed was a bunch of teenagers looking for somewhere to party and tell ghost stories. I was so upset at the disrespect for the people who were buried there. All I could think of was my grandma telling me, "You should always

show respect for the dead, never forget
that."

And so, we left, heavy hearted and angry
at what we had just seen. I couldn't undo
the wrongs that were done but I could

teach my nieces the same lesson that my grandma taught me. Respect. It seems to be a disappearing value in our society today. Respect for the elderly, respect for traditions, respect for different cultures, respect for authority and most of all respect for those who have passed away. As I told my nieces the values my grandma taught me, I could only hope that they would pass them on to their friends and someday their children too.

Made in the USA
Lexington, KY
18 April 2018